In schwindendem Licht

Spuren jüdischen Lebens im Osten Europas

In Fading Light

Traces of Jewish Life in the East of Europe

Christian Herrmann

Mit einem Vorwort von Adam Kerpel-Fronius

With a foreword by Adam Kerpel-Fronius

Lukas Verlag

Erstausgabe, 1. Auflage 2018

Lukas Verlag für Kunst- und Geistesgeschichte
Kollwitzstraße 57
D 10405 Berlin
www.lukasverlag.com

Bildbearbeitung: Christian Herrmann, Anita Nalewaja
Lektorat der englischen Texte: Karin Walker
Druck und Verarbeitung: argraf/Chromapress
Printed in EU

ISBN 978-3-86732-301-7

Dieses Buch wurde durch einen Druckkostenzuschuss von Klaus-Dieter L. Ehmke anlässlich seines 60. Geburtstags ermöglicht.

This book was made possible by a generous contribution to the printing costs from Klaus-Dieter L. Ehmke on the occasion of his 60th birthday.

VORWORT

von Adam Kerpel-Fronius

Für die meisten Europäer ist es heute so gut wie unmöglich, sich die Welt vorzustellen, wie sie vor nicht einmal hundert Jahren in Osteuropa war. Die dort einst blühende und sehr eigene, aber auch sehr heterogene jüdische Kultur wurde fast vollständig im Holocaust vernichtet. Die meisten Juden Osteuropas wurden ermordet: in den deutschen Vernichtungslagern auf dem Gebiet Polens, in rumänischen Lagern und Ghettos irgendwo in „Transnistrien" oder in der besetzten Sowjetunion bei Massenerschießungen direkt an den Orten, an denen sie lebten. Ihre Knochen befinden sich noch immer dort unter der Erde, in Tausenden von Massengräbern, die sich über dieses immense Gebiet von der Ostseeküste bis zum Schwarzen Meer erstrecken, das Timothy Snyder die Bloodlands nannte. Die meisten derjenigen, die überlebten und nach dem Blutvergießen in ihre Heimat zurückkehrten, entschlossen sich später ebenfalls zu gehen. Heute gibt es kaum noch Menschen, die sich noch an diese Welt erinnern können.

Für Reisende aus Westeuropa ist es dennoch erstaunlich, wie viele Spuren in Osteuropa nach wie vor vorhanden sind: Häuser, in denen Juden lebten, Synagogen, die heute als Kinos oder als Lagerhäuser genutzt werden, Friedhöfe, die oft verlassen und zugewachsen, aber weiterhin als solche erkennbar sind. Manchmal scheint es, als hätten die Einheimischen vergessen, dass diese Orte einst Wahrzeichen jüdischen Lebens waren, während in anderen Fällen die heutige Nutzung der verlassenen Gebäude einfach nur das Ergebnis pragmatischer Entscheidungen zu sein scheint, die nach dem Krieg aus der Not heraus geboren wurden – oder aus ideologischen Gründen in der atheistischen Sowjetunion. Natürlich ist dies keineswegs ein Phänomen, das es nur in Osteuropa gibt, auch anderswo sieht man ehemalige Synagogen, die unkenntlich sind. In Osteuropa ist es aber eben die schiere Zahl der heute noch sichtbaren Spuren, die so überwältigend ist.

Am Anfang war Christian Herrmann selbst ein solcher Reisender. In den 1990er-Jahren besuchte er Krakau zum ersten Mal. Er war fasziniert von der Stadt, vor allem auch von ihrem reichen jüdischen Erbe – Krakau war jahrhundertelang ein wichtiges Zentrum des europäischen Judentums gewesen. Seither kehrt er regelmäßig zurück und hat einen wesentlichen Teil seines Lebens dem Reisen durch Regionen wie Galizien, Bessarabien und der Bukowina gewidmet. Seine Kameras sind immer mit dabei. Er ist kein Berufsfotograf, aber er ist so gut wie einer geworden. Er sagt, dass er nicht nach einem Motiv gesucht, sondern dass das Motiv ihn gefunden habe.

Unzählige ehemalige Stätten jüdischen Lebens sind für immer verschwunden. Diese Leere ist eines von Herrmanns Themen. In Wolhynien beispielsweise gab es einst über 300 Synagogen, heute stehen nur noch etwa 30 der Gebäude in einem mehr oder weniger prekären Zustand. In einigen Fällen sind sogar ganze Ortschaften vom Erdboden verschwunden. Ein Beispiel dafür ist Trochenbrod, von dem Christian Herrmann ursprünglich annahm, dass es nur in Jonathan Safran Foers Roman *Alles ist erleuchtet* existierte. Aber wie will man die Leere einfangen, wie sollte man etwas fotografieren, das nicht mehr da ist? Das ist das Hauptinteresse von Christian Herrmann: Er kann die Toten nicht mehr zum Leben erwecken, aber er versucht sein Bestes, ihre Geister zu beschwören.

Eine weitere sehr starke Motivation für seine Arbeit ist die Tatsache, dass sich unsere visuelle Kultur in Bezug auf den Holocaust in fast extremer Weise auf einen einzigen Ort fokussiert – Auschwitz. Das Motiv mit dem berüchtigten Lagertor von Auschwitz-Birkenau und den Bahngleisen wurde bereits millionenfach fotografiert. Auschwitz ist zur Ikone des Holocaust geworden, aber es ist unmöglich und vor allem irreführend, den Holocaust auf einen einzigen Ort zu reduzieren. Was indes noch schwerer wiegt: Auschwitz ist zwar der Ort des Todes, aber es ist gleichermaßen wichtig, sich für die Orte zu interessieren, an denen die Opfer gelebt haben.

Natürlich ist Herrmann nicht der erste und nicht der letzte Fotograf des jüdischen Erbes Osteuropas. Der Titel seines Blogs *Vanished World* ist eine Hommage an den Fotopionier Roman Vishniac. Er, S. An-Sky, Alter Kacyzne und andere, die in der ersten Hälfte des 20. Jahrhunderts lebten, hatten die Möglichkeit, das Leben in den Straßen der Schtetl zu fotografieren. Die Kameratechnik war damals mobiler geworden und führte zu einem neuen Stil, den wir heute als Street Photograpy kennen. Nach dem Holocaust waren die jüdische Welt und ihre Bewohner weitgehend verschwunden. Seither sind es fast immer nur noch deren Spuren, die fotografiert werden können.

Einer der wichtigsten Wegbereiter Christian Herrmanns war David Goberman (1912–2003), der in den 1950er-Jahren begann, jüdische Grabsteine in der Ukraine und Moldawien abzulichten, ohne jegliche Hoffnung, seine Bilder in der Sowjetunion veröffentlicht zu sehen. In den 1970er-Jahren folgte der ungarische Holocaustüberlebende Lajos Erdélyi (*1929) aus Siebenbürgen, der eher zufällig verlassene jüdische Friedhöfe als Motiv entdeckte, während er auf einer Reise durch die Bukowina seiner Arbeit als Fotojournalist nachging.

In den 1980er-Jahren war es Monika Krajewska, die jüdische Friedhöfe in Polen fotografierte und in zwei Fotoalben veröffentlichte. Weitere, auf deren Schultern Christian Herrmann steht, sind Chris Schwarz, Andrzej Polec, Jason Francisco, Simon Geissbühler, Łukasz Baksik und Wojciech Wilczyk.

Christian Herrmanns Fotografie befindet sich irgendwo im Grenzgebiet zwischen Dokumentation und Kunst. Sein Stil ist ausgesprochen künstlerisch, aber seine Bilder werden auch wichtige Dokumente sein, wenn man später nachvollziehen will, in welchem Zustand sich das jüdische Erbe Osteuropas in den ersten Jahrzehnten des 21. Jahrhunderts befand. Diese Weltgegend ist keine Blackbox, die historische Spuren für immer konserviert. Im Gegenteil, die Landschaften verändern sich ständig, da diese Regionen eine Zeit der intensiven Modernisierung und des Wandels durchlaufen, manchmal zum Besseren, manchmal zum Schlechteren: Während die fantastische Große Synagoge von Drohobytsch restauriert wird, verfallen andere Gebäude zusehends und stürzen früher oder später unausweichlich ein.

Seit einigen Jahren nimmt das Interesse am jüdischen Osteuropa zu: Chassidische Juden pilgern zu den Gräbern ihrer Rabbis, Menschen aus aller Welt möchten die Orte ihrer Vorfahren erleben und auch die jüdischen Gemeinden vor Ort verzeichnen neue Aktivität. Glücklicherweise wächst überall in Europa das Bewusstsein dafür, dass die verbliebenen Spuren jüdischen Lebens integraler Bestandteil unseres gemeinsamen kulturellen Erbes sind. Doch am Ende kommt es auf die einzelnen Akteure vor Ort und ihre oft mühsame alltägliche Arbeit an, sie zu erhalten. Auf den letzten Seiten seines Buches lenkt Christian Herrmann die Aufmerksamkeit auf sie: jene Aktivisten, die das Leben in den jüdischen Gemeinden aufrechterhalten und sich für die Bewahrung des jüdischen Erbes einsetzen. Christian Herrmann leistet einen wichtigen Beitrag zu ihrer Sache, indem er das Bewusstsein für sie schärft und die einst verborgenen Schmuckstücke durch seine Fotos, seinen Blog *Vanished World* und nun endlich auch durch diesen großartigen Bildband bekannt macht.

Adam Kerpel-Fronius ist Historiker und arbeitet bei der Stiftung Denkmal für die ermordeten Juden Europas.

FOREWORD

by Adam Kerpel-Fronius

For most Europeans living today, it is almost impossible to imagine the world as it was in Eastern Europe less than a hundred years ago. The region's once thriving, very specific, but also highly heterogeneous Jewish culture was eradicated almost completely as a result of the Holocaust. Most Jews of Eastern Europe were murdered in German extermination camps on Polish territory or in Romanian camps and ghettos somewhere in "Transnistria". In the case of the occupied Soviet Union, the vast majority were killed in mass shootings right where they lived. Physically, their remains are still there in the ground, in thousands of mass graves scattered across an immense territory – "bloodlands", in the words of Timothy Snyder – stretching from the Baltic Sea coast to the Black Sea. Most of those who survived and returned home after the bloodshed decided, later, to leave after all. Today, there are hardly any more eyewitnesses to this world as it was.

For many a traveller from Western Europe, it is stunning how many traces are still present in Eastern Europe: Jewish places of residence; synagogues, now used as cinemas or warehouses; cemeteries, often abandoned and overgrown but still recognizable as such. Sometimes it seems the locals appear to have forgotten that these places were once landmarks of Jewish life, while in other cases, the repurposing of the abandoned buildings after the war may have been simply the result of pragmatic decisions born out of necessity – or, in the atheist Soviet Union, had ideological reasons. Of course, this phenomenon is in no way exclusive to Eastern Europe; there are plenty of examples of synagogues becoming unrecognizable elsewhere, too. What is different about Eastern Europe, though, is the sheer overwhelming number of visible traces of Jewish life.

Initially, Christian Herrmann was such a traveller. He first visited Kraków in the 1990s and was transfixed by the city but also by its rich Jewish heritage – for centuries, Kraków was an important centre of the European Jewry. He has been returning regularly ever since, dedicating a substantial part of his life to travelling through regions such as Galicia, Bessarabia and Bukovina. His cameras are always with him. Although not a professional photographer, he has all but become one. He says that he was not looking for an object at which to direct his lens; instead, the object found him.

Countless former sites of Jewish life are gone forever. This absence is one of Herrmann's topics. For instance, the town of Volhynia was once home to over 300 synagogues. Now, only around 30 of them still exist, most in precarious condition. In some cases, even whole towns have disappeared from the face of the earth. One such example is Trochenbrod, a former shtetl of which Christian Herrmann originally thought it only existed in Jonathan Safran Foer's novel *Everything is Illuminated*. But how does one capture absence? How does one take a picture of something that is no longer there? This is Christian Herrmann's main interest. He can't bring back the dead, but he tries his best to summon their ghosts.

Another powerful motivation for his work is the fact that when it comes to the Holocaust, our visual culture is almost exclusively centred on one individual site – Auschwitz. The infamous gate of Auschwitz-Birkenau and the railway tracks have been photographed millions of times. Auschwitz has become the icon of the Holocaust, yet it is impossible and more to the point, misleading to reduce the

Holocaust to any one place. More importantly, while Auschwitz is a site of death, it is equally important to care for the places where the victims lived.

Of course, Herrmann is neither the first nor the last to photograph Jewish heritage in Eastern Europe. The title of his blog, *Vanished World*, is a tribute to the photography pioneer Roman Vishniac. Vishniac, S. An-Sky, Alter Kacyzne and others contemporaries of the first half of the 20th century were still able to photograph capture life on the streets of the shtetls. Also, technical progress meant it was much easier to move around while carrying a camera, leading to a new style that would later be known as street photography. After the Holocaust, this Jewish world and its inhabitants virtually disappeared. Since then, in most cases the only motifs left to photograph are their traces.

One of the most important trailblazers for Christian Herrmann was David Goberman (1912—2003), who began photographing Jewish tombstones in Ukraine and Moldova in the 1950s without any hope of having his pictures published in the Soviet Union. In the 1970s, the Hungarian Holocaust survivor Lajos Erdélyi (*1929) from Transylvania followed suit, stumbling upon abandoned Jewish cemeteries almost by accident while travelling in Bukovina on a routine photo journalism assignment. In the 1980s, it was Monika Krajewska who photographed Jewish cemeteries in Poland and published them in two photo albums. Others on whose shoulders Christian Herrmann stands are Chris Schwarz, Andrzej Polec, Jason Francisco, Simon Geissbühler, Łukasz Baksik and Wojciech Wilczyk.

Christian Herrmann's photography is located somewhere along the border between documentary and art. His style is decidedly artistic, yet in future his pictures will bear valuable witness to the state of Jewish heritage in Eastern Europe during the early decades of the 21st century. These regions are not black boxes in which historical traces are preserved forever. On the contrary, the landscapes are changing constantly as these regions undergo a period of intense modernization and change. Change that is sometimes for the better, sometimes for the worse: while the incredible Great Synagogue of Drohobycz is being restored, other buildings are slowly decaying and are bound to collapse sooner or later.

For some years now, the interest in Jewish Eastern Europe has been increasing. Hasidic Jews make their pilgrimage to the tombs of their rabbis, people from all over the world travel to visit their ancestral towns, and local Jewish communities are engaging in fresh activities. Fortunately, there is now growing awareness everywhere in Europe that the remaining traces of Jewish life are an integral part of our common cultural heritage. Still, in the end it all comes down to individual actors on the ground and their often painstaking day-by-day work to preserve them. In the final sequence of his book, Christian Herrmann directs our attention to the activists who sustain life in the Jewish communities and are committed to preserving Jewish heritage. Herrmann is a major contributor to their cause in that he raises awareness of their work and makes these once hidden gems widely known through his photos, his blog *Vanished World* and now, at last, this beautiful album.

Adam Kerpel-Fronius is a historian working at the Foundation Memorial to the Murdered Jews of Europe.

Ich habe nichts zu sagen. Nur zu zeigen.

I have nothing to say. Just to show.

Walter Benjamin

Staryj Sambir, Galizien, Ukraine, 2017 | Ehemalige Synagoge

Staryi Sambir, Galicia, Ukraine, 2017 | Former synagogue

Pidhajzi, Galizien, Ukraine, 2017 | Ruine der Großen Synagoge

Pidhaitsi, Galicia, Ukraine, 2017 | Ruin of the Great Synagogue

Probischna, Galizien, Ukraine, 2017 | Ruine der Großen Synagoge

Probizhna, Galicia, Ukraine, 2017 | Ruin of the Great Synagogue

Kopytschynzi, Galizien, Ukraine, 2017 | Ehemaliges jüdisches Gemeindezentrum

Kopychyntsi, Galicia, Ukraine, 2017 | Former Jewish community centre

Kopytschynzi, Galizien, Ukraine, 2017 | Ehemaliges jüdisches Gemeindezentrum

Kopychyntsi, Galicia, Ukraine, 2017 | Former Jewish community centre

Klewan, Wolhynien, Ukraine, 2017 | Ruine der Großen Synagoge

Klevan, Volhynia, Ukraine, 2017 | Ruin of the Great Synagogue

Tirgul Vertiujeni, Bessarabien, Republik Moldau, 2016 | Verlassenes jüdisches Geschäft

Tirgul Vertiujeni, Bessarabia, Republic of Moldova, 2016 | Abandoned Jewish shop

Bibrka, Galizien, Ukraine, 2017 | Ruine der Großen Synagoge

Bibrka, Galicia, Ukraine, 2017 | Ruin of the Great Synagogue

Bibrka, Galizien, Ukraine, 2017 | Ruine der Großen Synagoge

Bibrka, Galicia, Ukraine, 2017 | Ruin of the Great Synagogue

Kischinau, Bessarabien, Republik Moldau, 2016 | Ruine der Leichenhalle auf dem jüdischen Friedhof

Chișinău, Bessarabia, Republic of Moldova, 2016 | Ruin of the mortuary at the Jewish cemetery

Raşcov, Bessarabien, Republik Moldau (abtrünnige Region Transnistrien), 2016 | Ruine der Großen Synagoge

Raşcov, Bessarabia, Republic of Moldova (breakaway region of Transnistria), 2016 | Ruin of the Great Synagogue

Nowoselyzja, Bessarabien, Ukraine, 2014 | Ehemalige Synagoge, vormals als Club einer kommunistischen Jugendorganisation zweckentfremdet

Novoselytsia, Bessarabia, Ukraine, 2014 | Former synagogue, formerly misappropriated as a Communist youth clubhouse

Tscherniwzi (Czernowitz), Bukowina, Ukraine, 2017 | Wandmalereien in der *Groissen Schil*, der Großen Synagoge im alten jüdischen Viertel

Chernivtsi, Bukovina, Ukraine, 2017 | Murals in the *Groisse Shil*, the Great Synagogue in the old Jewish neighbourhood

Tscherniwzi (Czernowitz), Bukowina, Ukraine, 2017 | Wandmalereien in der *Groissen Schil*, der Großen Synagoge im alten jüdischen Viertel

Chernivtsi, Bukovina, Ukraine, 2017 | Murals in the *Groisse Shil*, the Great Synagogue in the old Jewish neighbourhood

Lwiw, Galizien, Ukraine, 2016
| Spendenbüchse in der Jakob-Glanzer-Schul

Lviv, Galicia, Ukraine, 2016
| Donation box in the Jakob Glanzer Shul

צדקה
מתן

Lwiw, Galizien, Ukraine, 2015 | Ladenschild eines jüdischen Hutmachers

Lviv, Galicia, Ukraine, 2015 | Shop sign of a Jewish hatter

Lwiw, Galizien, Ukraine, 2017 | Ladenschild

Lviv, Galicia, Ukraine, 2017 | Shop sign

Sambir, Galizien, Ukraine, 2017 | Ladenschild

Tscherniwzi (Czernowitz), Bukowina, Ukraine, 2017 | Türdekoration einer ehemaligen jüdischen Wohlfahrtsorganisation in der Synagogengasse

Chernivtsi (Czernowitz), Bukovina, Ukraine, 2017 | Decorative element on the door of a former Jewish charity organisation in Synagogue Lane

Busk, Galizien, Ukraine, 2018 | Davidstern an der Tür der ehemaligen Großen Synagoge

Busk, Galicia, Ukraine, 2018 | Star of David on the door of the former Great Synagogue

Stryj, Galizien, Ukraine, 2017 | Ehemaliges jüdisches Viertel

Stryi, Galicia, Ukraine, 2017 | Former Jewish neighbourhood

Stryj, Galizien, Ukraine, 2017 | Spur einer Mesusa

Stryi, Galicia, Ukraine, 2017 | Trace of a mezuzah

Pidhajzi, Galizia, Ukraine, 2017 | Ehemaliges jüdisches Viertel

Pidhaitsi, Galicia, Ukraine, 2017 | Former Jewish neighbourhood

Pidhajzi, Galizia, Ukraine, 2017 | Spur einer Mesusa

Pidhaitsi, Galicia, Ukraine, 2017 | Trace of a mezuzah

Radechiw, Galizien, Ukraine, 2017 | Ehemalige jüdische Geschäfte und Häuser am Marktplatz

Radekhiv, Galizia, Ukraine, 2017 | Former Jewish shops and homes on the market square

Radechiw, Galizien, Ukraine, 2017 | Spur einer Mesusa

Radekhiv, Galizia, Ukraine, 2017 | Trace of a mezuzah

Kolomyja, Galizien, Ukraine, 2017 | Spur einer Mesusa

Kolomyia, Galicia, Ukraine, 2017 | Trace of a mezuzah

Lwiw, Galizien, Ukraine, 2014 | Spur einer Mesusa

Lviv, Galicia, Ukraine, 2014 | Trace of a mezuzah

Lwiw, Galizien, Ukraine, 2017 | Spur einer Mesusa

Lviv, Galicia, Ukraine, 2017 | Trace of a mezuzah

Lwiw, Galizien, Ukraine, 2017 | Spur einer Mesusa

Lviv, Galicia, Ukraine, 2017 | Trace of a mezuzah

Kolomyja, Galizien, Ukraine, 2017 | Spur einer Mesusa

Kolomyia, Galicia, Ukraine, 2017 | Trace of a mezuzah

Tschortkiw, Galizien, Ukraine, 2018 | Spur einer Mesusa

Chortkiv, Galicia, Ukraine, 2018 | Trace of a mezuzah

Warschau, Masowien, Polen, 2015 | Spur einer Mesusa

Warsaw, Masovia, Poland, 2015 | Trace of a mezuzah

Kolomyja, Galizien, Ukraine, 2017 | Spur einer Mesusa

Kolomyia, Galicia, Ukraine, 2017 | Trace of a mezuzah

Lwiw, Galizien, Ukraine, 2017 | Spur einer Mesusa

Lviv, Galicia, Ukraine, 2017 | Trace of a mezuzah

Wolotschysk, Podolien, Ukraine, 2017 | Aus einem Grabstein gefertigter Schleifstein auf dem jüdischen Friedhof

Volochysk, Podolia, Ukraine, 2017 | Grindstone made from a tombstone at the Jewish cemetery

Kischinau, Bessarabien, Republik Moldau, 2016 | Mauer aus jüdischen Grabsteinen auf dem christlichen Friedhof

Chișinău, Bessarabia, Republic of Moldova, 2016 | Wall made of Jewish tombstones at the Christian cemetery

Lwiw, Galizien, Ukraine, 2017 | Jüdischer Grabstein im Pflaster eines Hinterhofs

Lviv, Galicia, Ukraine, 2017 | Jewish tombstone used as a paving stone in a backyard

Tschabariwka, Galizien, Ukraine, 2017 | Jüdische Grabsteine im Fundament eines Stalls der ehemalige Kolchose „Kommunist“

Chabarivka, Galicia, Ukraine, 2017 | Jewish tombstones in the foundations of a stable at the former agricultural collective “Communist”

Tschabariwka, Galizien, Ukraine, 2017 | Ehemalige Kolchose „Kommunist"

Chabarivka, Galicia, Ukraine, 2017 | Former agricultural collective "Communist"

Rezina, Bessarabien, Republik Moldau, 2016 | Improvisierter Grillplatz auf dem jüdischer Friedhof

Rezina, Bessarabia, Republic of Moldova, 2016 | Improvised barbecue site at the Jewish cemetery

Horodenka, Galizien, Ukraine, 2015 | Ehemalige Große Synagoge, heute eine Sporthalle

Horodenka, Galicia, Ukraine, 2015 | Former Great Synagogue, now a gym hall

Busk, Galizien, Ukraine, 2015 | Ehemalige Große Synagoge, heute als Kirche und Wohnhaus genutzt

Busk, Galicia, Ukraine, 2015 | Former Great Synagogue, now used as a church and apartment building

Tscherniwzi (Czernowitz), Bukowina, Ukraine, 2015 | Ehemaliger Israelitischer Tempel, heute ein Kino

Chernivtsi (Czernowitz), Bukovina, Ukraine, 2015 | Former Israelitic Temple, now a cinema

Radechiw, Galizien, Ukraine, 2017 | Ehemalige Große Synagoge, heute Teil einer Werkstatt

Radekhiv, Galizia, Ukraine, 2017 | Former Great Synagogue, now part of a workshop

Rosdil, Galizien, Ukraine, 2017 | Ruine der Großen Synagoge, heute ein Lagerraum

Rozdil, Galicia, Ukraine, 2017 | Ruin of the Great Synagogue, now a warehouse

Sbarasch, Galizien, Ukraine, 2017 | Ehemalige Große Synagoge, heute eine Wodka-Destillerie

Zbarazh, Galicia, Ukraine, 2017 | Former Great Synagogue, now a vodka distillery

Câmpulung Moldovenesc, Bukowina, Rumänien, 2015 | Ehemalige Synagoge, heute eine Bar

Câmpulung Moldovenesc, Bukovina, Romania, 2015 | Former synagogue, now a bar

Berehowe, Transkarpatien, Ukraine, 2018 | Ehemalige Große Synagoge, heute ein Kulturhaus

Berehove, Transcarpathia Ukraine, 2018 | Former synagogue, now a cultural centre

Sambir, Galizien, Ukraine, 2017 | Ehemalige Große Synagoge, heute ein Fitness-Center

Sambir, Galicia, Ukraine, 2017 | Former Great Synagogue, now a gym

Komarno, Galizien, Ukraine, 2017 | Ehemalige jüdische Schule, heute ein Geschäft

Komarno, Galicia, Ukraine, 2017 | Former Jewish school, now a shop

Luzk, Wolhynien, Ukraine, 2017 | Ehemaliges Lehrhaus der Chassidim von Olyka, heute Teil einer Busstation

Lutsk, Volhynia, Ukraine, 2017 | Former Beit Midrash of Olyka Hasidim, now part of a bus station

Luzk, Wolhynien, Ukraine, 2014 | Ehemalige Große Synagoge mit angebauter Sporthalle

Lutsk, Volhynia, Ukraine, 2014 | Former Great Synagogue with gym hall attached

Boryslaw, Galizien, Ukraine, 2018 | Ehemaliges Lehrhaus, heute eine Werkstatt

Boryslav, Galicia, Ukraine, 2018 | Former Beit Midrash, now a workshop

Zgurița, Bessarabien, Republik Moldau, 2016 | Jüdischer Friedhof

Zgurița, Bessarabia, Republic of Moldova, 2016 | Jewish cemetery

Berdytschiw, Podolien, Ukraine, 2017 | Zerstörter jüdischer Friedhof, heute ein öffentlicher Park

Berdychiv, Podolia, Ukraine, 2017 | Destroyed Jewish cemetery, now a public park

Chyriw, Galizien, Ukraine, 2017 | Zerstörter jüdischer Friedhof, heute ein Kindergarten und ein Spielplatz

Khyriv, Galicia, Ukraine, 2017 | Destroyed Jewish cemetery, now a kindergarten and playground

Strij, Galizien, Ukraine, 2017 | Zerstörter Jüdischer Friedhof, heute ein Bauhof

Stryi, Galicia, Ukraine, 2017 | Destroyed Jewish cemetery, now a builder's yard

Busk, Galizien, Ukraine, 2015 | Unmarkiertes Massengrab

Busk, Galicia, Ukraine, 2015 | Unmarked mass grave

Misotsch, Wolhynien, Ukraine, 2016 | Zerstörtes ehemaliges Ortszentrum

Mizoch, Volhynia, Ukraine, 2016 | Destroyed former town centre

Trochenbrod, Wolhynien, Ukraine, 2015 | Ehemaliges Zentrum des zerstörten Ortes

Trochenbrod, Volhynia, Ukraine, 2015 | Former centre of the destroyed town

Misotsch, Wolhynien, Ukraine, 2016 | Ort einer Massenerschießung

Mizoch, Volhynia, Ukraine, 2016 | Mass shooting site

Slawuta, Wolhynien, Ukraine, 2017
| Ort einer Massenerschießung

Slavuta, Volhynia, Ukraine, 2017 |
Mass shooting site

Lwiw, Galizien, Ukraine, 2017 | Massengräber beim ehemaligen Konzentrationslager an der Janowska-Straße

Lviv, Gaicia, Ukraine, 2017 | Mass graves next to the former concentration camp on Yanovska Street

Mykolaiw, Galizien, Ukraine, 2017 |
Planiertes Massengrab

Mykolaiv, Galicia, Ukraine, 2017 |
Bulldozed site of a mass grave

Krakau, Polen, 2014 | Gelände des ehemaligen Konzentrationslagers Płaszów

Kraków, Poland, 2014 | Site of the former Płaszów concentration camp

Turka, Galizien, Ukraine, 2017 | Denkmal für die ermordeten Juden des Ortes auf dem zerstörten jüdischen Friedhof

Turka, Galicia, Ukraine, 2017 | Memorial for the murdered Jews of the town at the destroyed Jewish cemetery

Turka, Galizien, Ukraine, 2017 | Zerstörter jüdischer Friedhof

Turka, Galicia, Ukraine 2017 | Destroyed Jewish cemetery

Raliwka, Galizien, Ukraine, 2017 | Massengräber

Ralivka, Galicia, Ukraine, 2017 | Mass graves

Lwiw, Galizien, Ukraine, 2018 | Massengräber im Wald des Vororts Lysynytschi

Lviv, Galizia, Ukraine, 2018 | Mass graves in the forest near the suburb of Lysynychi

Warschau, Masowien, Polen, 2018 | Jüdischer Friedhof im Stadtteil Bródno

Warsaw, Masovia, Poland, 2018 | Jewish cemetery in Bródno district

Karzcew, Masowien, Polen, 2017 | Jüdischer Friedhof

Karczew, Masovia, Poland, 2017 | Jewish cemetery

Bălţi, Bessarabien, Republik Moldau, 2016 | Jüdischer Friedhof

Bălţi, Bessarabia, Republic of Moldova, 2016 | Jewish cemetery

Bereschany, Galizien, Ukraine, 2017 | Jüdischer Friedhof

Berezhany, Galicia, Ukraine, 2017 | Jewish cemetery

Staryj Sambir, Galizien, Ukraine, 2014 | Jüdischer Friedhof

Staryi Sambir, Galicia, Ukraine, 2014 | Jewish cemetery

Budapest, Ungarn, 2018 | Jüdischer Friedhof an der Kozma-Straße

Budapest, Hungary, 2018 | Jewish cemetery on Kozma Street

Kalusch, Galizien, Ukraine, 2017 |
Jüdischer Friedhof

Kalush, Galicia, Ukraine, 2017 |
Jewish cemetery

Făleşti, Bessarabien, Republik Moldau, 2016 | Jüdischer Friedhof

Făleşti, Bessarabia, Republic of Moldova, 2016 | Jewish cemetery

Gura Humorului, Bukowina, Rumänien, 2015 | Jüdischer Friedhof

Gura Humorului, Bukovina, Romania, 2015 | Jewish cemetery

Orhei, Bessarabien, Republik Moldau, 2016 | Jüdischer Friedhof

Orhei, Bessarabia, Republic of Moldova, 2016 | Jewish cemetery

Suceava, Bukowina, Rumänien, 2015 | Jüdischer Friedhof im Vorort Itcani

Suceava, Bukovina, Romania, 2015 | Jewish cemetery in the suburb of Itcani

Kischinau, Bessarabien, Republik Moldau, 2016 | Jüdischer Friedhof

Chișinău, Bessarabia, Republic of Moldova, 2016 | Jewish cemetery

Vadul-Raşcov, Bessarabien, Republik Moldau, 2016 | Jüdischer Friedhof

Vadul-Raşcov, Bessarabia, Republic of Moldova, 2016 | Jewish cemetery

Vadul-Raşcov, Bessarabien, Republik Moldau, 2016 | Jüdischer Friedhof

Vadul-Raşcov, Bessarabia, Republic of Moldova, 2016 | Jewish cemetery

Siret, Bukowina, Rumänien, 2015 |
Neuer Jüdischer Friedhof

Siret, Bukovina, Romania, 2015 |
New Jewish Cemetery

Kischinau, Bessarabien, Republik Moldau, 2016 | Porträt eines Jungen auf dem Neuen Jüdischen Friedhof

Chişinău, Bessarabia, Republic of Moldova, 2016 | Portrait of a boy at the New Jewish Cemetery

Tscherniwzi (Czernowitz), Bukowina, Ukraine, 2014 | Porträts auf einem Grabstein auf dem jüdischen Friedhof

Chernivtsi (Czernowitz), Bukovina, Ukraine, 2014 | Portraits on a tombstone at the Jewish cemetery

Soroca, Bessarabien, Republik Moldau, 2016 | Im Inneren der Synagoge

Soroca, Bessarabia, Republic of Moldova, 2016 | Interior of the synagogue

בשמחת
תורה

Soroca, Bessarabien, Republik Moldau, 2016 | Synagoge

Soroca, Bessarabia, Republic of Moldova, 2016 | Synagogue

Soroca, Bessarabien, Republik Moldau, 2016 | Gemeindeaktivist
Semen Veksler

Soroca, Bessarabia, Republic of Moldova, 2016 | Community activist
Semen Veksler

Soroca, Bessarabien, Republik Moldau, 2016 | Im Inneren der Synagoge

Soroca, Bessarabia, Republic of Moldova, 2016 | Interior of the synagogue

Dorohoi, Bukowina, Rumänien, 2015 | Synagoge, restauriert mithilfe eines Programms der Europäischen Union

Dorohoi, Bukovina, Romania, 2015 | Synagogue, restored using European Union funds

Botoșani, Moldau, Rumänien, 2015 | Synagoge, restauriert mithilfe eines Programms der Europäischen Union

Botoșani, Moldavia, Romania, 2015 | Synagogue, restored using European Union funds

Schowkwa, Galizien, Ukraine, 2016 | Innenansicht der Großen Synagoge, nach dem Krieg teilweise wiederaufgebaut

Zhovkva, Galicia, Ukraine, 2016 | Interior of the Great Synagogue, partly reconstructed after the war

Schowkwa, Galizien, Ukraine, 2016 | Großen Synagoge

Zhovkva, Galicia, Ukraine, 2016 | Great Synagogue

Lwiw, Galizien, Ukraine, 2015 | Jakob-Glanzer-Schul, ein im Aufbau befindliches jüdisches Kulturzentrum

Lviv, Galicia, Ukraine, 2015 | Jakob Glanzer Shul, a Jewish cultural centre under construction

Lwiw, Galizien, Ukraine, 2016 | Innenansicht der Jakob-Glanzer-Schul, ein im Aufbau befindliches jüdisches Kulturzentrum

Lviv, Galicia, Ukraine, 2016 | Interior of Jakob Glanzer Shul, a Jewish cultural centre under construction

Lwiw, Galizien, Ukraine, 2017 | Sascha Nazar und Freiwillige des Lviv Volunteer Center bergen jüdische Grabsteine aus einem Hinterhof

Lviv, Galicia, Ukraine, 2017 | Sasha Nazar and volunteers from the Lviv Volunteer Center salvage Jewish tombstones from a backyard

Lwiw, Galizien, Ukraine, 2017 | Bei Straßenbauarbeiten entdeckte jüdische Grabsteine, die während der deutschen Besatzung als Straßenpflaster verbaut wurden

Lviv, Galicia, Ukraine, 2017 | Jewish tombstones discovered during roadworks, which were misused during the German occupation as paving slabs

Rohatyn, Galizien, Ukraine, 2017 | Fragmente von Grabsteinen aus Baustellen, die von lokalen Aktivisten zum alten jüdischen Friedhof zurückgebracht wurden

Rohatyn, Galicia, Ukraine, 2017 | Fragments of tombstones from a construction site returned by local activists to the old Jewish cemetery

Berdytschiw, Wolhynien, Ukraine, 2017 | Jüdischer Friedhof, chassidische Pilgerstätte

Berdychiv, Volhynia, Ukraine, 2017 | Jewish cemetery, Hasidic pilgrimage site

Berdytschiw, Wolhynien, Ukraine, 2017 | Jüdischer Friedhof, chassidische Pilgerstätte

Berdychiv, Volhynia, Ukraine, 2017 | Jewish cemetery, Hasidic pilgrimage site

Brazlaw, Podolien, Ukraine, 2015 | Synagoge, chassidische Pilgerstätte

Bratslav, Podolia, Ukraine, 2015 | Synagogue, Hasidic pilgrimage site

Budapest, Ungarn, 2017 | Jüdischer Friedhof an der Salgótarjáni-Straße

Budapest Hungary, 2017 | Jewish cemetery on Salgótarjáni Street

Krakau, Polen, 2014 | Alter jüdischer Friedhof

Kraków, Foland, 2014 | Old Jewish cemetery

Tscherniwzi (Czernowitz), Bukowina, Ukraine, 2014 | Jüdischer Friedhof, seit 2008 ein Ort von zivilgesellschaftlichen Initiativen zu seinem Erhalt

Chernivtsi (Czernowitz), Bukovina, Ukraine, 2014 | Jewish cemetery, since 2008 the focus of civil society preservation initiatives

Tscherniwzi (Czernowitz), Bukowina, Ukraine, 2014 | Jüdischer Friedhof

Chernivtsi (Czernowitz), Bukovina, Ukraine, 2014 | Jewish cemetery

Tscherniwzi (Czernowitz), Bukowina, Ukraine, 2014 | Leichenhalle auf dem jüdischen Friedhof

Chernivtsi (Czernowitz), Bukovina, Ukraine, 2014 | Mortuary of the Jewish cemetery

Tscherniwzi (Czernowitz), Bukowina, Ukraine, 2014 | Stiftertafel in der Leichenhalle des jüdischen Friedhofs

Chernivtsi (Czernowitz), Bukovina, Ukraine, 2014 | Donors' plaque at the mortuary of the Jewish cemetery

Über den Autor

Christian Herrmann (*1962) lebt in Köln und arbeitet für eine Non-Profit-Organisation in Bonn. Seit Jahren bereist er Osteuropa auf der Suche nach Spuren jüdischen Lebens. Aus den Bildern entstehen Ausstellungen und Bücher. Seine Erlebnisse dokumentiert er in seinem Blog „Vanished World“, ein Online-Archiv, das beständig fortgeschrieben wird.

Ich möchte denjenigen Menschen danken, ohne die dieses Buch nicht möglich gewesen wäre. Klaus-Dieter L. Ehmke, der die Veröffentlichung großzügig unterstützt hat. Frank Böttcher, der als Verleger einsprang, als die Herausgabe bereits aussichtslos erschien. Ich danke meinen lieben Freunden und Reisegefährten Joachim Steinigeweg, Petra Lutz, Vasyl Yuzyshyn, Marla Raucher Osborn, Jay Osborn und allen, die meine Reisen virtuell begleitet haben und mir mit Rat und Tat zur Seite gestanden haben. Ihr alle wisst, wer Ihr seid.

https://vanishedworld.blog

About the author

Christian Herrmann (*1962) lives in Cologne and works for a non-profit organisation in Bonn. For years he has been travelling in search of the traces of Jewish life in Eastern Europe. The images are used for exhibitions and books. He documents his experiences in his blog “Vanished World”, an online archive that is constantly updated.

I would like to thank the people who made this book possible: first and foremost Klaus-Dieter L. Ehmke, who generously supported the publication, and Frank Böttcher, who stepped in as a publisher when publication seemed hopeless. I would also to thank my dear friends and fellow travellers Joachim Steinigeweg, Petra Lutz, Vasyl Yuzyshyn, Marla Raucher Osborn, Jay Osborn and all those who have accompanied my travels virtually and who have helped with words and deeds. You all know who you are.